Learning and Study Skills Program Level II

Teacher's Guide

Third Edition

Developed by
The hm Study Skills Group

Author and Senior Editor:
David Marshak

Editorial Board:
Kiyo Morimoto
and Jerome A. Pieh

ScarecrowEducation
Lanham, Maryland • Toronto • Oxford
2000

Published in the United States of America
by ScarecrowEducation
An imprint of The Rowman & Littlefield Publishing Group, Inc.
4501 Forbes Boulevard, Suite 200, Lanham, Maryland 20706
www.scarecroweducation.com

PO Box 317
Oxford
OX2 9RU, UK

Our thanks to all of the thousands of teachers, students, counselors, and administrators who used the first two editions of the Level II Program and contributed their suggestions to us; and particularly to five talented educators who aided in this revision: Jackie Sage-Phillips, William F. Faulkner, Andy Hansen, Kay l. Puma, and Jack Ogden.

The three step study method in Unit V is loosely adapted from the SQ3R Method in *Effective Study* by Francis P. Robinson. Copyright 1941, 1946 by Harper and row Publishers, Inc. Copyright 1961, 1970 by Francis P. Robinson. Reprinted by permission of Harper and Row Publishers, Inc.
British Library Cataloguing in Publication Information Available

ISBN 0-8108-3803-6 (pbk. : alk. paper)

The paper used in this publication meets the minimum requirements of American National Standard for Information Sciences—Permanence of Paper for Printed Library Materials, ANSI/NISO Z39.48-1992. Manufactured in the United States of America.

TABLE OF CONTENTS

INTRODUCTION TO THE hm LEARNING AND STUDY SKILLS PROGRAM: LEVEL II

The **hm Learning and Study Skills Program: Level II** is designed to provide you with a valuable resource for the teaching of learning and study skills. Please read this Introduction carefully so you can gain a sense of the purposes and values, the means and ends, and the capacities and limitations of this **Program**.

Please note that this is the third edition of the **hm Learning and Study Skills Program: Level II.**

LEARNING AND STUDY SKILLS: WHAT ARE THEY?

Learning and study skills are methods for acquiring knowledge, understanding, and competence. A look at the listing of units in this **Program** will give you examples of important learning and study skills, such as listening, taking notes, and time use.

In this literal sense, learning and study skills involve specific, observable behaviors that can be described and measured. For example, can a student attend to a set of directions and follow them accurately? Can a student plan the use of his or her study time and follow that schedule? Can a student take useful notes from an oral presentation? Can a student read a section of text and identify the main ideas and important details?

There is also a more profound definition of learning and study skills than this literal one. In this larger sense, learning and study skills are processes for learning. They are processes that help students to organize and direct the effort they invest in learning, and their use results in students becoming more effective and efficient learners who are more in charge of their own learning. When students master a skill for learning, they are learning more than just a technique. They are learning a way of solving learning problems, a method of approach and follow-through that can be used in any relevant context. They are also learning more about how to learn effectively. It is this larger understanding of learning and study skills that reveals their central role in schooling.

LEARNING SKILLS AND STUDY SKILLS: WHAT'S THE DIFFERENCE?

Many educators equate the terms *learning skills* and *study skills*. Others see a shade of difference in their meanings, with study skills referring primarily to school-based learning and learning skills referring to learning in any context. In this third edition of the **hm Study Skills Program: Level II**, we have chosen to join these terms together so that we can emphasize our belief that the skills for learning are critical in any learning context: in school, at home, in post-secondary education, and in the workplace.

As we restructure and re-invent our secondary schools for the needs of our students in the 21st century, we are coming to understand that students must be active, meaning-seeking and meaning-making learners. Learning and study skills are among the tools that students need to be able to use well as they engage in their meaning-seeking and meaning-making activities.

LEARNING AND STUDY SKILLS, AND INDEPENDENT LEARNING

One key element on the agenda of most school change efforts in this decade is the encouragement of students' effectiveness as independent learners. When students develop a repertoire of learning skills, they become more independent as learners. For example, students who know how to analyze a problem and develop and use a strategy for its solution will be able to proceed with this task whether or not the teacher is available. Students who have mastered an array of learning and study skills will be able increasingly to take charge of their own learning.

Students develop learning and study skills best when they have an opportunity to try a variety of study methods and procedures, decide which ones are most effective for them, and gradually refine these methods and strategies into a personal study system.

THE hm LEARNING AND STUDY SKILLS PROGRAM: LEVEL II

The **hm Learning and Study Skills Program: Level II** is designed to provide *an introduction to learning and study skills* for 8th, 9th, and 10th grade students through a series of twelve activity-oriented units. Many of the units can be completed in one conventional period of class time. Some will require more than a single period.

The **hm Program** is structured on the assumption that activity-oriented lessons are the most effective instructional strategy for the teaching of study skills: more succinctly, that "learning by doing" is the best way to master learning and study skills.

The **hm Learning and Study Skills Program: Level II** is *not* remedial in character. Rather, it is designed to assist students at most levels of competence in their development of essential learning and study skills, and to reinforce already existing skills.

The **Program** is deliberately designed to address a wide range of student needs:

1. For the student who has little sense of a particular skill, it provides an introduction to the skill.

2. For the student who is ready to acquire initial competence in a skill, it provides a learning experience.

3. For the student who has already mastered a skill, participation in one of the **Program's** lessons offers review, reinforcement, and the opportunity to increase one's level of competence in that skill.

Thus, the **Program** allows for the participation of students with a wide range of skills and promotes learning on various levels of competence.

The **hm Program: Level II** provides you with a focus on the nature and value of learning and study skills. It gives you twelve initial instructional units dealing with a variety of crucial skills. In addition, it offers you suggestions for additional instruction related to the various skills.

The **hm Learning and Study Skills Program: Level II** can serve as a workbook for classroom use. After the completion of the last unit, students should be allowed to keep their **Programs,** so the **Program** can be a resource and handbook to which they can refer throughout the same school year and subsequent ones. Or, **Programs** may be re-used as needed.

The **hm Learning and Study Skills Programs** include the following:

The **hm Study Skills Program: Level A** . . . . for grades 1-2
The **hm Study Skills Program: Level B** . . . . for grades 3-4
The **hm Study Skills Program: Level I** . . . . for grades 5-7
The **hm Learning and Study Skills Program: Level II** . . . . for grades 8-10
The **hm Learning and Study Skills Program: Level III** . . . . for grades 11-13
The **hm Math Learning and Study Skills Program**. . . . . for grades 6-10
The **hm Science Learning and Study Skills Program** . . . . for grades 7-10
The **hm Study Skills Inventory 1** . . . . for grades 4-7
The **hm Study Skills Inventory 2** . . . . for grades 8-12

Parents Guide to Learning and Study Skills English or Spanish

TEACHING THE hm STUDY SKILLS PROGRAM: LEVEL II

Developing Learning And Study Skills: Trial And Error

People learn skills through processes of repeated trial and error. One key to learning and study skills teaching, then, is providing students with sufficient opportunity for practice of the skill to be learned. The **hm Learning and Study Skills Program: Level II** includes only one practice of each skill that it introduces. If your students are to master the study skills presented by this **Program**, it is essential that you provide them with structured and ongoing opportunities for practice of the various skills. For example, we know of teachers who have selected four or five learning skills that they judged to be of the greatest value in their courses and have focused their instruction on these in the weeks and months after their initial use of the entire **Program**.

Of course, there is an inevitable tension between providing your students with trial and error practice of a new learning skill and helping your students to maintain their interest in learning the skill in the face of the necessary repetition. While this tension cannot be willed away, we are confident that you can minimize it by using variation and imagination in your instructional design. For example, if your students are learning to take notes, let them practice their skills in a wide variety of contexts and for many different purposes. Also, as your students practice a new learning and study skill, help them to see the benefits that they will gain from their increasing mastery of the skill.

Learning From Errors

A second key to teaching learning and study skills is the recognition that learning a study skill requires the learner to err before he or she can succeed. We learn skills by being presented with a new skill, trying to use that skill ourselves, committing errors, identifying our errors and learning from them, and then correcting them. The understanding of this process of learning skills creates several responsibilities for the teacher:

a. The teacher must provide a space within the learning process where students can try out a new skill, experience a good deal of error, but not feel that they have failed or are "failures."

b. The teacher must provide usable feedback to students about the effectiveness of their use of the new learning skill.

c. The teacher must provide students with enough opportunities for practice of the new skill, so the students begin to master the skill and discover that they can now do what they could not do before.

d. The teacher must reward students for what they have done well in using the new learning skill. With such recognition, students experience success in the learning process, validated both by their own new ability and by the teacher's recognition of this. The experience of success motivates students to continue the development of mastery of the new study skill.

Learning And Study Skills, And Learning Style

Research in cognitive and learning styles during the past three decades has demonstrated what perceptive classroom teachers have known for a long time: people learn in very different and personal ways. Thus, learning and study skills should not be taught in a rigid and prescriptive manner that indicates to students that all individuals ought to develop exactly the same repertoire of skills. Rather, as is appropriate to their level of maturity, students need to be involved in a self-reflective process whereby they learn more about their own learning styles while they are learning specific learning skills. Instruction that is guided by an awareness of individual differences in learning style will help students to develop learning and study skills that are specifically useful to their capacities, needs, and desires.

The **hm Learning and Study Skills Program: Level II** is grounded in an awareness of the importance of learning style as a powerful factor in all learning, including the learning of study skills. The **Program** introduces the concept of learning style to students in the "Introduction" and raises learning style issues as is appropriate throughout its twelve units.

Where To Teach The **hm** Learning And Study Skills Program

The learning skills included in the **hm Learning and Study Skills Program: Level II** are ones that are useful in the study of almost every subject. Thus, this **Program** can be successfully taught within the context of any subject with the exception, perhaps, of mathematics. (The **hm Math Learning and Study Skills Program** provides a learning skills resource for the mathematics classroom.) We have observed the effective use of the first two editions of this **Program** in social studies, English, science, and reading classes. We have also seen parts of it put to good use in home economics, foreign language, industrial arts and vocational training, and even physical education classes.

Building Learning And Study Skills Instruction Into The Curriculum

We strongly recommend that you teach the units from the **hm Learning and Study Skills Program** within the context of an already existing course rather than in a mini-course or homeroom setting. Only in the regular classroom can the teacher of the **hm Program** integrate learning and study skills with the curriculum of her or his course and help the student to see both the immediate and long-term value of mastering and employing learning skills.

Pacing Of The hm Program

Our evaluation of the classroom use of the first two editions of this **Program** has informed us that there is no single pacing for the teaching of the units that we can recommend. Rather, we have learned that teachers must pace the use of these units in a way that helps their own students learn and begin to master the various learning and study skills.

Some of the pacings that have been used effectively by classroom teachers include:

a.   One unit per week over a twelve week period;

b.   A division of the instructional responsibility for the units in the **Program** among different subject area teachers, with each one teaching some part of the **Program**;

c.   Three or four units in a one month period; then, a second month for ongoing practice of these skills, followed by the use of another three or four units in a one month period; and so on;

d.   One unit every 3-4 weeks over the length of most of the school year.

We suggest that you adopt an instructional strategy for learning skills that is suited to the needs of your students. We strongly recommend that you design a strategy that will provide opportunity for the immediate application and reinforcement of the various learning and study skills that students can learn through this **Program**.

Using Small Groups In The Classroom

For several units in the **hm Program**, we recommend the use of small, cooperative groups of students in working the various exercises. We do this for the following reasons:

a.   The interactions within small groups of students working on a common task can facilitate the learning of skills through shared problem solving. In this way students can share their talents and experience and learn from each other.

b.   Small group processes offer a superb method of genuinely engaging students in an activity. Such processes help both to enhance motivation for learning and to increase interest in the content of a lesson, because they offer active participation to each and every student.

You may wish to select the membership of the small groups based upon your knowledge of your students.

Of course, individual work is of critical importance to the learning of study skills. When a skill is introduced in a group setting, it becomes crucial to provide for individual work with that skill through homework and/or other class activities.

Using The hm Learning And Study Skills Program: Suggested Directions, Suggested Times, and Unit Summaries

Suggested Directions

The Teacher's Guide offers "Suggested Directions" for the teaching of each unit in the **Program**. Our classroom testing and observation has shown these methods to be useful. Of course, we invite you to adapt them in ways which you see fit.

We suggest that you examine both the Student Text and the Teacher's Guide carefully prior to your teaching of the various units.

The **Program** offers a content with which your students may practice the various skills. We invite you to substitute the content of your course in its place if you find this to be desirable.

THE CONTENT INCLUDED IN THIS **PROGRAM** IS COMPLETE WITH TWO EXCEPTIONS:

a.   In Unit I, Exercise I (page 13 in the Teacher's Guide) asks you to prepare and deliver a short talk.

b.   In Unit IV, Exercise I (page 28 in the Teacher's Guide) asks you to prepare and deliver a short talk. In the same unit, Exercise II (page 28 in the Teacher's Guide) asks you to prepare and lead a short class discussion.

The reason we ask you to participate in this way is discussed on page 11 of the Teacher's Guide.

NOTE that Unit II requires a decision on your part about how to use the various exercises included in this unit. See page 17 in the Teacher's Guide.

NOTE that Unit XII includes the only homework assignment for students in the **Program** that must be completed prior to the teaching of this unit. See page 55 in the Teacher's Guide.

Suggested Times

The "Suggested Directions" in the Teacher's Guide includes "approximate times" suggested for each activity or group of activities in each unit. These times are estimates based on the observation of a variety of classroom uses of these units. As noted above, many of the units in the **Program** are designed to fit into a single class period.

However, both our testing experience and classroom observation of the use of the first two editions of this **Program** have shown us that the wide variation in teaching style results in an equally wide variation in the pacing of instruction. We strongly suggest that you examine the **Program's** units carefully and gauge your planning of instructional time according to your knowledge of how things actually work in your classroom.

Unit Summaries

Each unit includes a summary as its final page. These unit summaries are included both in the Student Text and the Teacher's Guide. While the use of the summaries has not been included in the suggested directions for instruction, you will want to bring the unit summaries and their possible uses to the attention of your students.

Student Perceptions And Expectations

Sometimes students perceive new learning and study skills as more time consuming than their unskilled learning behaviors. In a few cases, this is an accurate perception, but most often it is not.

You can help students gain a wider perspective about their own learning by telling them that any skill, by its very nature, takes more time to use when you are first learning how to do it. Then, as you become more competent in using the skill, it takes less and less time. Ask students to think of examples of this from their own experience. Or, give them a few examples that will illustrate this relationship between competence and time.

Grading And The hm Learning And Study Skills Program

Given the grade-oriented reality of most schools, we suggest that students' involvement with the **hm Program** be graded in some fair and concrete manner. We propose an outcome-based approach for this grading, which is informed by the process of how skills are learned - through repeated practice over time - and which sets reasonable levels of expected mastery. With outcome-based grading, students' grades result not from each practice with the skill but from the level of mastery that students achieve in that skill at the end of a certain amount of time.

We also suggest that you inform your students about how their work with the **hm Program** will be evaluated at the very beginning of their use of the **Program**.

Additional Comments

The **hm Learning and Study Skills Program** is designed to be taught by a teacher in a classroom setting. It is not programmed material that students can work through by themselves, although some of the units can be used on an individual basis.

The **hm Program** incorporates as much student activity as possible, including individual, small group, and whole class activities. This emphasis results from our conviction that people learn skills best by doing.

It's important to note that the **hm Program** can also serve as a diagnostic tool for your use. An inspection of your students' working of the various units will provide you with specific information about their learning skills competencies. It will show you clearly what they already know and on what you need to focus your instructional attention.

We strongly recommend that you provide your students with an overview concerning the values and purposes of learning and study skills both in your classroom and throughout their lives.

AN IMPORTANT OMISSION: USING SCHOOL RESOURCES

Throughout our development of the first two editions of the **hm Program: Level II**, we considered the inclusion of units related to students' use of school resources. Two key resources in our view were (1) the school library or media center, and (2) the guidance and special services personnel. Eventually we decided not to include units of this sort, because we could not direct them specifically enough to the situation in your school.

We have reached the same decision for this third edition for essentially the same reasons. Again we urge you to examine carefully your students' needs for skills in gaining access to and using school resources and to provide your students with the necessary instruction for developing them, if they are not receiving such instruction in another context.

TEACHING THE "INTRODUCTION" TO THE STUDENT TEXT

The "Introduction" (pages 1-3 in the Student Text) to the **hm Learning and Study Skills Program: Level II** is designed to give your students an initial awareness of what learning and study skills are and what their value can be.

The "Introduction" also presents the concept of learning style and engages your students in a brief exploration of their own style of learning. While this concept is complex, students in grades 8-10 can understand it and can use the idea of learning style to help them better evaluate their own strengths and limitations as learners.

Please note: The "Introduction" will probably not require an entire class period. We recommend that you teach Unit I on the day after you have worked with the "Introduction."

SUGGESTED DIRECTIONS FOR THE INTRODUCTION

1. Give your students a brief overview of the **hm Learning and Study Skills Program** (what learning and study skills are included; how much time you will devote to the **Program** and how the **Program** will relate to the rest of your curriculum; what value you see in developing learning and study skills; how work done by students in connection with the **Program** will be graded). Then pass out the **Programs** to your students. Read "What Are Learning And Study Skills?" (page 1), "What Is The Value Of Learning And Study Skills?" (page 1), and "Learning Skills And Study Skills: What's The Difference?" (page 1) aloud to your students, or have individual students read sections of this aloud. Discuss each section for emphasis.

    Approximate time: 7-10 minutes

2. Ask a student(s) to read "Learning Style" (page 2) and the directions for Exercise I (page 2) aloud to the class, or have students read it to themselves. Go over the concept of learning style and discuss as is appropriate. Then ask your students to complete the exercise. You may want to help them begin to respond to the question asked in Exercise I. When they have completed the exercise, have them form small groups of three and share their responses with each other for a few minutes. Then gather the class together. Ask for questions, and provide any necessary clarification about the meaning of learning style.

    10-15 minutes

3. Read "Learning And Study Skills, And Learning Style" (page 3) aloud to your students, or have a student read it aloud. Emphasize the need for repeated practice in the mastery of learning and study skills. Also, explain that people learn new skills through processes of trial and error. Give your students "permission to make mistakes" when they begin to work with a new learning skill. Tell them that what's important is not that they make mistakes - everyone makes mistakes when they are learning - but that they learn from their mistakes.

    5-7 minutes

UNIT I
LEARNING TO LISTEN

Listening means more than just hearing. Listening means hearing and trying to understand and/or appreciate what you have heard.

In the primary grades, teachers are usually aware of listening as a learning skill and language art as important to effective communication as reading, writing, and speaking. Yet in secondary schools, teachers often seem to assume that students have already developed effective listening skills. This assumption is continually contradicted by the very real difficulties that many students have in listening effectively. If you feel at all skeptical of this conclusion, think about how many times each day you ask your students to listen more carefully. Or, how many times have students you've taught limited the success of their learning or achievement by not listening well?

The listening skills of secondary students need nearly as much instructional attention as those of their younger counterparts. Unit I presents an initial lesson that defines listening as a learning and study skill and engages students in beginning to learn several specific active listening skills.

Please note that Exercise I (page 6) asks you to create a short talk that you present to your class. The content for this is not provided, because this activity will be more engaging to your students if the talk is a part of your ongoing curriculum.

SUGGESTED DIRECTIONS FOR UNIT I

1. Note that the first learning skill in the **Program** is listening, in "Unit 1: Learning To Listen." Explain that you are going to involve your students in an exercise to see how carefully they listen. Have them open their **Programs** to page 4. Then ask the "Questions For Good Listeners" below, directing your students to write their responses on the lines provided (page 4 in the Student Text). Ask each question only once (or twice, if that seems more appropriate for your class). Tell students to expect this.

Questions For Good Listeners

1. Do they have a fourth of July in France?

2. Why can't a woman living in Lexington, Kentucky be buried west of the Mississippi?

3. A farmer in Montana had forty sheep. In a blizzard, all but nine died. How many does he have left?

4. Is it legal in California for a man to marry his widow's sister?

5. Some months have 31 days. Some have 30. How many have 28?

6. A plane crashed on the border between the United States and Mexico, in fact, right in the middle of the Rio Grande. In which country would the survivors be buried?

Answers:

---

1. Yes
2. A woman who is living can't be buried.
3. Nine

4. A man who has a widow is dead.
5. Twelve
6. Survivors are alive.

Go over the answers orally, and explore why people get wrong answers using one of the alternative procedures described below. (Many or most students will get some or many of the answers wrong.)

a) Give the correct answer to the first question. Have students who got the wrong answer raise their hands to show how widespread the errors are. (You may want to omit the show of hands if many of your students are not able to admit errors without embarrassment or disruption. If you do so, ask for a few volunteers who made errors to respond to the questions in the following sentence.) Then ask these students, "What made you go wrong with this one?" or "What led you to make that mistake?" On the board, list all of the causes of listening errors that your students offer.

You may also want to have a few students who got the correct answer share their process of listening. Ask them, "In what ways did you listen so that you got the answer right?"

Some students will probably note that these are "trick" questions. Stress the idea that even though they are "trick" questions to some extent, they are useful because, in an exaggerated way, they show common mistakes that people make in listening.

Repeat this process with each question, and discuss the causes of listening errors that are cited frequently.

b) Put the list of "Common Causes of Listening Errors" on the board. Then go through the questions in the same way as suggested above. Rather than asking students to explain their own causes of listening error, have them find the causes of their errors on the list. Discuss the various causes of listening errors.

Common Causes of Listening Errors

a) Focusing on a single word rather than on an entire question or sentence.

b) Jumping to a conclusion based on your expectations rather than what's actually been said.

c) Not understanding or paying attention to key words.

d) Switching the order of words.

e) Not noticing verb tense or other indications of when something happened.

Approximate time: 12-18 minutes

12

2. Have your students read "Listening Is A Skill" (page 4) and "Why Is It Hard To Listen Even When You're Interested?" (page 4), or have students read these sections aloud. Discuss briefly for emphasis. Then have your students read "How Can You Become An Active Listener?" (page 5) and "What Else Can You Do To Improve Your Listening Skills?" (page 5), or have several students read these sections aloud. Emphasize the specific skills of active listening.

    Some of your students may not be able to "picture" in their mind's eye. Studies indicate that while most of the people in grades 8-10 can see inner imagery or "pictures," part of this population cannot. We suggest that you only mention this to your class after they have done the exercise, so as to avoid creating any negative expectations among your students. Seeing inner imagery is a capability that some people have without being conscious of it. A negative expectation can lead them to ignore their own images if the first ones are not vivid.

    10-12 minutes

3. Before class, prepare a 5-7 minute talk that relates to the ongoing curriculum in your class. Include 2 or 3 main ideas in your presentation.

    Have your students read the directions for Exercise I (page 6). Then present your talk. When you have finished, ask your students to respond to the questions in Exercise 1. When they have done so, use one of the following options:

    a) Have your students form small groups of three. Ask them to share their responses with each other and discuss them. When they have had a few minutes to do this, gather the class and review the responses to each of the questions.

    b) Collect the **Programs**, and give your students written feedback about the quality of their responses. Then discuss this exercise with your class when you return the **Programs**. (If you choose this option, you will want to cover "Listening And Learning Style" (page 7) when you return the **Programs** to your students.)

    10-20 minutes

4. Have your students read "Listening And Learning Style" (page 7), or have a student read it aloud. Give students an opportunity to consider each of the questions. If you have time, you may wish to ask your students to share their responses to the questions with a partner. Discuss this concept as is appropriate.

    5-8 minutes

13

ADDITIONAL SUGGESTIONS

1. Teaching effective listening skills requires an ongoing effort. Below are suggestions for other kinds of instruction in effective listening. These suggestions are organized into three categories.

    Listening for information and organization

    A. The Message Game

        On paper, write a message that is 20-25 words long. You can use the example below or create your own.

        Explain the rules of the game to your students, as follows: you will whisper the message to a student; the first student will whisper it to the second, the second to the third, and so on, until the message goes around the class and reaches the last student; each person can state the message only once (or twice, if that is more appropriate for your class).

        Begin the game by whispering the message to the first student. When the last student receives it, ask her or him to write it on the board. At the same time, write the original message on the board next to it.

        Discuss how the message has changed. Focus on what role ineffective listening has played in this change.

        You may want to vary this exercise as follows:

        *   If your class is large and/or your students are impatient, set up two or three simultaneous message chains.

        *   Have each student write down the message she or he receives. Then reconstruct how the message changed as it was passed through the class.

        *   While the message is being passed, engage your students in a discussion to distract them from the whispering of the message. For example, discuss the role that attention plays in active listening.

        *   Have students write their own 20-25 word passages. Use one or several of them in this exercise.

        EXAMPLE OF A MESSAGE:

        Although Vanessa walked to Walmart today to buy a record for her brother, Victor, his birthday isn't until the week after next.

    B. Write a narrative paragraph in which the sequence of events is out of order. Read this paragraph aloud to your students, and ask them to re-order the sequence of events so that the paragraph makes sense. Have them write their re-ordering on paper. Have several volunteers read what they have written. Then discuss how difficult or easy this task was and which listening techniques were useful in doing it well.

C. Read a set of directions aloud twice. Then have students write the directions down. Have several students read aloud what they have written, and discuss how listening skills can help in making sense of directions.

You can also read a complex set of directions aloud to students, and ask them to create a list of the key steps in the directions. Students can do this individually or in pairs or trios.

D. Chain Stories

In this game, one student in each small group begins to tell a story. After three sentences, the next student continues the story for another three sentences, and so on. Each continuation of the story must be coherent with what has preceded it.

Divide your class into small groups of 4-6. Explain the rules of the game. Have a student in each group begin. Give students about 5 minutes to develop their stories. Then discuss what took place in each group with the whole class. Focus on the role of listening in this process. If you have time, repeat the procedure.

E. Introduce your students to common patterns of organizing material, for example, chronological order, compare/contrast, and cause and effect. Give short oral presentations to your students that employ these patterns, and help your students gain an awareness of how their recognition of a presentation's pattern of organization can help them to listen more effectively.

Critical listening

A. Read aloud a passage with a number of irrelevancies. Have your students identify the irrelevancies.

B. Read aloud a passage that includes both fact and opinion. Have your students distinguish between fact and opinion.

If they do not already understand this distinction, you will need to engage them in instruction that helps them learn to draw it.

Listening for appreciation

A. Have students listen to various forms of spoken language, i.e., plays, poetry, comedy, etc. Include listening activities as a regular part of your curriculum, so students become accustomed to listening skillfully and well both for learning and enjoyment. You can also include a critical element in this kind of activity by asking questions such as the following after the listening activity: "What do you like about what you have just listened to? How could you have listened in a better way?"

B. Have students close their eyes and listen to the sounds of their classroom environment for a few minutes. Then ask them to list all the sounds they heard. Have students share their lists and discuss them.

2. Once your students have read the "listen first, judge later" suggestion, you may want to elaborate on it by sharing something like the following:

> "Many people find that when they start to listen to someone, a voice comes into their head which says, "He's dumb" or "This is stupid." This kind of quick judgment gets in the way of good listening. Give people a chance! Good listening means putting away the negative thoughts many people have when they first begin to listen to another person. Good listening means really paying attention to what another person is saying."

Discuss these ideas with your students.

UNIT I SUMMARY: LEARNING TO LISTEN

Listening is a skill. It takes effort and practice to learn how to be a good listener.

The key to being a good listener is to be an active listener. How do you become an active listener?

1. While you listen, ask yourself questions about what the speaker is saying. Then try to answer your questions.

2. Try to "picture" what you are hearing in your mind's eye.

3. Regularly summarize what the speaker has already said.

4. Look at the person who is speaking. Try to establish eye contact.

5. Listen first, judge later. Don't try to evaluate what you are hearing until you've heard what the person has to say.

6. Take notes if you need to remember what's been said.

UNIT II
VOCABULARY: GETTING MEANING FROM CONTEXT

"Getting meaning from context clues" is the vocabulary learning and study skill of examining context to develop a working definition for an unknown or unfamiliar word. The use of this skill is associated both with students who are academically successful and with people who value and enjoy reading.

The addition of this study skill to the repertoire of 8th, 9th, and 10th graders will help to increase the effectiveness of their reading for learning and enjoyment. When they encounter an unknown word, many students choose either to ignore it or to disrupt the flow of their reading by looking it up at that moment. When students can use context clues to develop some understanding of the word, their process of reading can continue without interruption and will offer greater involvement, meaning, and reward. Then they can look up the word at an appropriate later time if desired.

The exercises in this unit increase in difficulty from Exercise I through Exercise IV. From our classroom testing, we have learned that students respond most enthusiastically to the activities of this unit when they are asked to begin working the exercises at a level that is neither too easy nor too difficult, one that challenges but still offers success. We suggest that you examine the exercises carefully prior to your use of them and select an appropriate starting point for your students. For example, if most of your students would not be sufficiently challenged until Exercise III, you may wish to cover Exercises 1-11 briefly and then have your students begin working Exercise III.

The items in Exercises V-Vl range throughout the spectrum in terms of difficulty but tend towards the more difficult end of that spectrum.

Please note that some of the examples of context clues included in this unit are somewhat exaggerated and probably unlike what a student will encounter in most prose. This exaggeration is used for the purpose of making the concepts presented as clear as possible. You may want to mention this to your students.

You may also wish to bring your students' attention to the caution that "getting meaning from context" is a highly useful but at times limited tool, that some or many words that they will encounter in their reading will not appear with enough context clues for this method to be fruitful.

SUGGESTED DIRECTIONS FOR UNIT II

1. Organize your class into small groups of 3-4 students.

2. Have students read the "Introduction" (page 8), or have a student read it aloud. Read "Getting Meaning From Context Clues" (page 8) aloud, or have students read it aloud. Clarify and emphasize the concepts "context" and "context clues." Ask your students to do the example at the bottom of page 8 on their own. Go over the answer to the example, and discuss the process of "getting meaning from context." Then read "Kinds Of Context Clues" (page 9) to your students.

    Approximate time: 10-14 minutes

3. For exercises on pages 9-12 that you decide your students do not need to complete:

    Ask a student to read aloud the description of the particular kind of context clue. Clarify as necessary. Ask your students to do the example on their own. Then go over the example. Repeat this procedure with the first item in the exercise.

    4-8 minutes for each exercise

4. For exercises on pages 9-12 that you will ask your students to complete:

    Read aloud the description of the particular context clue, or have a student read it aloud. Clarify as necessary. Ask your students to do the example on their own. Then go over the example. Have your students complete the items in the exercise as a group effort. When your students are ready, go over the exercise. Focus your discussion on the process of using context clues to create a working definition for an unknown word.

    8-14 minutes for each exercise

5. Ask your students to read "Hints For Using Context Clues" (page 13). Discuss for emphasis.

6. Exercise V (pages 13-14) and Exercise VI (pages 15-16) can be used for additional class work and/or homework.

7. Ask your students to read "A Final Hint About Context Clues" (page 17). Discuss for clarity.

    3-5 minutes

ANSWERS FOR EXERCISES IN UNIT 11

Accept any reasonable answer. The definitions below are suggested answers.

Example: incessant - continuing without stopping

Page 9

Example (definition): depreciate — lose value
Example (restatement): propaganda — spreading of narrow and often false views

Exercise I (circled words)
1. exact copy
2. taking it apart piece by piece
3. braced framework made of wood
4. proposed explanation for an event

Page 10

Example (example): sweatshop — place of work characterized by overcrowding, poor heat and ventilation, no fire escapes, and very low wages
Example (description): procrastinate — to delay action repeatedly

Exercise II
1. person who decides what others may read, watch, etc.
2. animals with backbones
3. geometrical forms with four sides
4. make less pure

Page 11

Example (comparison): predicament — difficult or trying situation
Example (contrast): demoted — lowered

Exercise III
1. a crowd
2. daring and skill
3. complete failure
4. no longer useful

Page 12

Example (inference): trepidation — fear

Exercise IV
1. friendly, usually with others
2. something that eases without curing
3. winding
4. shutting out outsiders, resisting letting others be a part of

Pages 13-14

Exercise V

1. unmoving
2. hired soldiers
3. a watch kept over a person
4. hatred or disgust
5. to make gestures with speech
6. pertaining to breathing
7. person requesting a favor or benefit
8. speak badly of
9. to see the differences between
10. frugal, careful with money
11. no longer in existence
12. lack of energy, weariness
13. express emotion or feeling
14. difficult problem or choice
15. something that angers or irritates

Pages 15-16

Exercise VI

1. a group of attendants and aides
2. scientist who studies birds
3. blocking the passage of light
4. strength and endurance
5. being strongly attracted to someone whom you don't know well and, as a result, acting unwisely or foolishly
6. to bring someone back from unconsciousness or apparent death
7. brothers and sisters
8. being alone
9. to sail all the way around
10. small, slight
11. loss of memory
12. word for word
13. intoxicated, drunk
14. composed of widely different kinds of parts or elements
15. place where bees are kept

ADDITIONAL SUGGESTIONS

1. You may find it valuable to create more exercises similar to Exercises V and VI in this unit. Completing these exercises will give your students more practice with this skill.

2. Help your students begin to understand that the context for an unknown or unfamiliar word can be not just the surrounding words and phrases but its entire paragraph or even more. Provide your students with examples of this larger kind of context clue, and give them opportunities to practice "getting meaning from context" where the context is a paragraph or more.

3. Select passages from texts in a variety of subject areas, both at the grade level of your students and at levels a year or two higher their current grade. Identify difficult words from these passages, and engage your students in trying to develop understandings of these words from the context clues in the passages. Particularly with text passages that are above the grade level of your students, you may want to engage them in this kind of activity as a challenge or small group competition.

4. In small groups, have your students select an unfamiliar word from the dictionary. Have them discuss the meaning of this unfamiliar word, so they have developed an understanding of it. Ask them to write a paragraph including this word. Have them make sure that the paragraph includes context clues that make the unfamiliar word's meaning apparent. When they are ready, have each group switch paragraphs with another group. Then have each group figure out the meaning of the unknown word from context clues.

5. You may want to engage your students in a discussion of and work with the concepts of "in context" and "out of context" as they relate both to reading and to the particulars of your subject.

6. Engage your students in exercises like the one below that can help them to see that the same word can have many different meanings in differing contexts.

   Directions: Figure out the meaning of the word "head" as it is used in each context in the sentences below. Write each meaning in the blank at the right of each sentence.

   Example:

   Why is your sister standing at the *head* of the stairs?   _____

   1. Mrs. Gandhi was the *head* of her government in India for more than ten years.   _____

   2. The "cheap" movie charged four dollars a *head* for the double feature on Saturday night.   _____

   3. If you pour a bottle of beer directly into a glass and not along its side, you can create a *head* of two or three inches in the glass.   _____

21

4. Regretfully he told his teacher that Chemistry just seemed
    to be over his *head*.   _____

5. The old man was wearing a battered brown derby on his *head*. _____

6. They grew more than thirty *heads* of lettuce in their garden. _____

7. The usher allowed the mayor to go right to the *head* of the line. _____

8. The *head* of the Mississippi River lies up in north central _____
    Minnesota.

7. Write several pairs of sentences in which the same unknown word is used. In one sentence of the
    pair, include a context clue. In the other, do not. Share these with your students, and discuss the
    differences.

UNIT II SUMMARY: VOCABULARY: GETTING MEANING FROM CONTEXT

One good way to figure out the meaning of an unknown word is to use *context clues*.

The *context* is the setting in which the unknown word is found — the words, phrases, and sentences
around it. Context clues are familiar words and phrases. From the meaning of these, you can often
figure out the meaning of the unknown word.

The kinds of *context clues* are:

1. Definition or restatement

    The context actually includes a definition of the unknown word. Or, the context gives you a
    restatement of it, expressing its meaning in other words.

2. Example or description

    The context includes examples of the unknown word that can give you an idea of its meaning.
    Or, the context describes the meaning of the unknown word.

3. Comparison or contrast

    The context tells you what the unknown word is like or what it's not like.

4. Inference

    The context gives you enough information about the unknown word so that you can draw
    some reasonable conclusions about, or infer, its meaning.

When you read, try to use *context clues* to gain a sense of the meaning of an unknown or
unfamiliar word. Then look up the unknown word in the dictionary when you come to a natural
break in your reading. See how close your context definition is to the dictionary definition.

UNIT III
NOTE TAKING METHODS

Effective note taking is perhaps the single most useful learning and study skill that students can develop. The ability to take good notes will prove very helpful not only in every academic context but also in any situation in which students need to read or hear a presentation, evaluate its contents as to their importance, and create a useful record of its main ideas and details. The process of taking notes results in learning both when the notes are initially created and later whenever they are used.

What is central to note taking instruction is its ends, not its means. The purpose of such instruction is to help students learn a reliable method(s) for taking useful notes. There are a variety of techniques that students can use toward this end. This unit introduces two of these note taking methods:

> outlining, and
> mapping — a pictorial approach that is described below.

Both methods are introduced through their application to written materials. Unit IV provides practice in applying these methods to oral presentations.

To take notes effectively, students must have the ability to identify main ideas and important, supporting details within a written or oral presentation. The level of instruction in Units III and IV assumes that your students have already developed at least a rudimentary skill in identifying main ideas and supporting details. If many or some of your students do not have this skill yet, you will want to provide them with the instruction necessary for its development. Unit IX in the **hm Study Skills Program: Level I** will give you a model for teaching/learning processes of this kind. Unit III in the **Level I Program** may also be helpful to you, as it includes instruction in categorizing, a skill very much related to the identification of main ideas and important details.

MAPPING: WHAT IS ITS VALUE?

Research into learning styles during the past three decades has verified what every perceptive classroom teacher already knows: that people perceive, understand, and respond to the world in very different and personal ways. The evidence of these individual differences we can see every day in the ways our students express their thinking and feeling.

This understanding of diversity in perception, cognition, and feeling is a useful concept to apply to the teaching of note taking methods. While some students are comfortable with the outline form, others can only struggle with its demands, especially when the presentation that they are experiencing lacks an obvious order.

Mapping is an alternative note taking method that can prove extremely useful (1) to students for whom outlining is not a helpful tool, and (2) in situations where the presentation lacks a clear organization, such as class discussion. Mapping requires less organization than outlining does as a student goes along but results in almost equally well-organized notes. Although it may be used in any context, mapping is particularly helpful for taking notes during unstructured oral presentations.

Certainly outlining is an important and useful note taking method. Mapping can also be useful to your students, particularly to those who find outlining difficult. Although mapping may be new to you, we suggest that you examine it carefully, experiment with its applications, and help your students master its uses if you share our perception of its value.

If you are interested in learning more about mapping, we suggest that you examine *Using Both Sides of Your Brain* by Tony Buzan (New York: E.P. Dutton, 1976, 1990).

OTHER NOTE TAKING METHODS

You may want to introduce your students to additional note taking methods beyond mapping and outlining. A number of methods use a two column structure.

1. In the Cornell Method, the student draws lines on the page to create a wide left margin (about a third of the page) and a small summary section at the bottom of the sheet. The student uses the right section of the page for taking notes with any method chosen by the student. Then, on the same day as the notes were taken, the student reviews the notes and identifies key words, concepts, and questions, which are jotted down in the left margin. At the bottom of the page, the student writes a concise summary of all the material noted above.

2. Another two-column method uses the left margin for questions and the right section of the page for answers. A variation on this approach uses the left margin for main ideas and the right section for details.

SUGGESTED DIRECTIONS FOR UNIT III

1. Have a student read "Why Take Notes?" (page 18) aloud, or read it aloud yourself. Discuss briefly. Emphasize the purposes of note taking and the concept of notes as "a map of ideas and information." Then have a student read "Note Taking Methods" (page 18) aloud.

    Approximate time: 8-10 minutes

2. Ask your students to read "Outlining" (page 19) and Paragraph I (page 19). Discuss the "Outline for Paragraph I" (page 19), focusing both on the form of the outline and on what is included in it and omitted from it. Have students read "How To Outline" (page 20), "Formal Outlines And Informal Outlines" (page 20), and "Tips For Taking Notes" (page 20), or read these sections aloud. Discuss the differences between formal and informal outlines and when each form might be appropriate. Then ask your students to do Exercise I (page 21) in pairs or individually. When they have done so, go over the exercise. Have several students write their outlines on the board. Then evaluate and discuss their outlines.

    14-20 minutes

3. Have your students read "Mapping" (page 22) and "Paragraph II" (page 22), focusing on the form of the map. Ask your students to read "How To Map" (page 23). Then have your students do Exercise II (page 23) in pairs. When your students have done so, go over the exercise. Ask several students to write their pair's map on the board. Evaluate and discuss these maps.

    14-20 minutes

4. Ask your students to do Exercise III (pages 24-25). If your students are not familiar with the concept of a sequence, you will need to explain it to them. You may want to give your students the choice of completing this exercise by working alone or in pairs. When your students are ready, go over the exercise. Have several students write their maps on the board. Evaluate and discuss them. Also, discover how many different ways your students created to note a sequence in a map. Stress the notion that there is no single correct method for indicating a sequence, that the only question is whether the method works or not.

    8-12 minutes

5. You may want to work through "Using Abbreviations And Symbols In Note Taking" (page 26) and Exercise IV (page 26) in class. Or, assign them for homework. In either case, go over Exercise IV in class.

    You may want to note to your students that while abbreviations of the kind included in this exercise are very helpful for taking notes, they are not usually acceptable usage for formal writing.

    8-10 minutes

6. Read "Taking Useful Notes" (page 27) aloud to your students, or have a student read it aloud. Discuss briefly, focusing on the value of learning at least one note taking method that works well for you as an individual learner.

    5-8 minutes

ANSWERS FOR EXERCISES IN UNIT III

Page 21

Exercise I
I. Women had few rights in 1800s
    A. Property of father, husband
    B. No vote or government office holding
    C. Considered inferior
    D. Starting winning rights 1900s in most states

Page 23

Exercise II

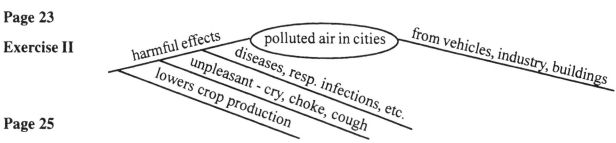

Page 25

Exercise III
Answers will vary. Accept any answers that clearly note the sequence of metals described in the passage.

Page 26

Exercise IV
Answers will vary. Accept any answers that students can explain clearly.

ADDITIONAL SUGGESTIONS

1. To help your students develop a mastery of outlining and/or mapping, you will need to provide them with ongoing practice in the use of these note taking skills. You will also need to offer them ways of receiving feedback about the quality of their notes both from their peers and from yourself. The best way to accomplish these goals is to integrate ongoing note taking assignments into your curriculum. Also, on a regular basis, give students an opportunity to evaluate each others' notes in small groups and to receive feedback about their notes from you. Through this kind of ongoing process, you can both help students see for themselves the value of taking notes and keep your students engaged in improving their note taking skills.

    A few ways to integrate note taking instruction into your curriculum include:

    *   Give assignments on which students can use their notes and clearly benefit from having taken them.

    *   Give "open note" quizzes and tests.

    *   Engage students in evaluating and discussing each others' notes in pairs or small groups.

    *   Go over students' notes with the whole class as a way of reviewing main ideas.

2. Exercise III gives your students practice in mapping a sequence. You may want to give them an opportunity to use mapping with other patterns of organization. For example: cause and effect, compare and contrast.

3. Once your students have gained an initial competence in taking notes, you will want to engage them in considering the purposes of their note taking. For example, it is likely that someone would take different notes from a reading according to what her or his purpose is in taking these notes.

    One exercise that allows students to explore the relationship between the purpose of their note taking and the actual notes that they write is the following:

    Give students a short piece of reading from which notes can be taken for different purposes. Then ask your students to read the passage and take notes for several different purposes. For example:

    *   What notes would you take from this passage if you were preparing for a test?

    *   What notes would you take from this passage if you thought you might want to come back to this topic and learn more about it later on?

    *   What notes would you take from this passage for your own information?

    *   What notes would you take from this passage if you had to make a brief oral report about it?

    Give students an opportunity to share and discuss their responses to questions like these. Stress the idea that they will want to fit the kinds of notes they take to their purpose for note taking in any situation.

4. Once your students have become comfortable with using abbreviations and symbols, suggest that they may find it useful to keep a list for themselves of the abbreviations and symbols that they use. The more abbreviations and symbols that they use in their notes, the more helpful this kind of list will be.

UNIT III SUMMARY: NOTE TAKING METHODS

Taking notes helps you to learn in two ways:

1. To take good notes, you need to figure out what the important ideas and details are in what you're reading or hearing. Figuring out what these important ideas and details are and then writing them down will help you to learn them.

2. You can use your notes a week or a month later to study for a test.

Think of your notes as a MAP. Write down only the main ideas and important details. Also, be sure to write your notes in your own words.

Two good methods for taking notes are:

1. OUTLINING -- FORMAL   INFORMAL

    I. Main idea   1. Main idea
       A. Supporting detail   a. Detail
       B. Supporting detail   b. Detail
          1. Sub-detail   c. Detail -- sub-detail
          2. Sub-detail

2. MAPPING

Use abbreviations and symbols as much as possible when you take notes. The more you can use them, the less writing you'll have to do, and the more time you will have for reading and listening.

UNIT IV
LISTENING AND TAKING NOTES

This unit provides your students with an opportunity to integrate listening skills and note taking skills. Its activities engage students in applying active listening and both note taking methods, outlining and mapping, to oral presentations.

Please note that the activities in this unit will only introduce your students to the integrative use of these active listening skills and note taking skills. For your students to master employing active listening and note taking skills together, you'll need to build ongoing practice with these skills into your curriculum.

This unit calls on you to create and deliver a short lecture and to organize and lead a short class discussion. As in the first unit, we have left the content of these activities to your discretion.

SUGGESTED DIRECTIONS FOR UNIT IV

1. Have several students read aloud the "Introduction" (page 28), "Why Take Notes In Class?" (page 28), "How Do You Start?" (page 29), and "What To Keep In Mind About Listening And Taking Notes?" (page 29). Discuss each section briefly after it has been read. Emphasize the choices that students need to make as presented in "How Do You Start?" Also, you may want to review the active listening skills in more detail than what is given in "What To Keep In Mind About Listening And Taking Notes?"

    Approximate Time: 8-12 minutes

2. Before this class, create a 4-6 minute lecture. Put a brief outline for this lecture on the board (or write the outline on the board as you deliver the lecture). Ask your students to read the directions for Exercise I (page 30). Then deliver the lecture. Have your students take notes in outline form from your presentation. At the conclusion of the lecture, (1) have students gather in small groups and share their notes with each other; after a period of small group discussion, gather the whole class and engage students in describing what they noticed about the various sets of notes. (2) Or, at the conclusion of the lecture, have several students write their notes on the board. Engage the class in discussing and evaluating these sets of notes.

    You may want to record your lecture prior to class and play the recording at the appropriate time. This will allow to observe your students' note taking more carefully.

    14-22 minutes

3. Before this class, prepare for a short class discussion. Have your students read the directions for Exercise II (page 31). Conduct a 4-8 minute class discussion. Ask your students to take notes in mapping form about this discussion. At the conclusion of the discussion, (1) have students gather in small groups and share their notes with each other; after a period of small group discussion, gather the whole class and engage students in describing what they noticed about the various sets of notes. (2) Or, at the conclusion of the discussion, have several students write their notes on the board. Engage the class in discussing and evaluating these sets of notes.

    If appropriate, select a controversial topic for discussion, so the discussion will be lively.

    14-22 minutes

ADDITIONAL SUGGESTIONS

1. To help your students gain mastery in listening and taking notes, you will need to engage them in the same kind of ongoing instruction and practice described in the "Additional Suggestions" for Unit III.

2. Organize your students into small groups. Engage them in an activity like Exercises I and II in this unit. Once students have taken notes from this oral presentation, ask a volunteer in each group to reconstruct that presentation orally from his or her notes. Ask the other group members to give him or her feedback about the reconstruction.

UNIT IV SUMMARY: LISTENING AND TAKING NOTES

Taking brief notes in class can help you to learn both when you first write the notes down and when you use them for studying.

1. You can use the outline method to take notes for a lecture or any kind of organized presentation.

2. You can use the mapping method to take notes for any class activity that is less organized, such as a class discussion.

3. If you feel particularly comfortable with any one way of taking notes, use the method whenever you can.

Remember to be an active listener!

UNIT V
A WAY TO READ TEXTBOOKS

In this era of increasing reliance on computer-based information systems, textbooks still play an important role in many secondary classrooms, either as a central curricular source or as one resource among many. In either situation most students have few skills that they can use for learning effectively and efficiently from textbook reading.

The purpose of this unit is to give your students a simple and effective method for reading textbooks and learning from that activity. The method presented is a variation of F. P. Robinson's SQ3R (survey, question, read, recite, and review). The method presented here — **survey, read and take notes, review** — is designed to offer students a way to learn from textbooks systematically and efficiently, and to experience textbook reading as engaging and purposeful.

SUGGESTED DIRECTIONS FOR UNIT V

1. At the beginning of the period, organize your class into pairs.

2. Ask your students to read the "Introduction" (page 33) and complete Exercise I (page 33) individually. When they have done so, list a variety of student responses on the board. Discuss for emphasis.

    Approximate time: 6-10 minutes

3. Read aloud "How Do You Read A Textbook?" (page 33) and "A Way To Read Textbooks" (pages 34-35), or have several students read these sections aloud. Discuss each step in the textbook reading method for emphasis.

    10-12 minutes

4. Ask your students to do Exercise II (pages 35-36) with their partners. When they have completed the exercise, have several pairs write their notes on the board. Evaluate the sets of notes and discuss the **survey, read and take notes, review method**. You may wish to elicit from your students both benefits and problems they see in the use of this method.

    12-18 minutes

5. Have several students read "What Are The Advantages Of The Survey, Read And Take Notes, Review Method?" (page 37) and "Tips For Taking Notes From Your Reading" (page 38) aloud. Discuss briefly for emphasis.

    5 minutes

6. Have students do Exercise III (pages 38-39) in their pairs. Or, assign Exercise III for homework. In either case, go over students' notes in class by having several students put their notes on the board and discussing how they constructed their notes. Then involve students in discussing their experience of using the **survey, read and take notes, review method**.

    12-18 minutes

ANSWERS FOR EXERCISES IN UNIT V

Page 33

Exercise I

These are suggested responses:

1. Textbooks present and explain information. Novels and short stories tell a story.

2. Textbooks are organized into chapters and sections, with chapter titles and section headings. Novels usually only have chapters. Short stories don't have either.

3. Textbooks usually include additional materials to help you learn, such as diagrams, maps, pictures, summaries, review questions, etc. Novels and stories don't usually include these.

4. Textbooks are written to teach the reader. Novels and short stories may also attempt to teach but must first involve the reader in a story.

Page 36

Exercise II

Suggested notes:
I. Auto - new way to travel
   A. Internal combustion engine, developed in Europe
   B. First American cars - 1890s
   C. Best cars gas powered

II. Changes brought by cars
   A. Very major industry created
   B. System of paved roads
   C. Accidents -- people hurt, killed

Page 39

Exercise III

Suggested notes:

I. Flying machines
   A. First airplane - 1903 - Wright brothers
   B. 1700s - balloons
   C. 1800s - wooden gliders

II. Aviation (science of building and flying airplanes) improves
   A. Mechanics built better planes
   B. World War I - new uses for planes
   C. 1927 - Lindbergh flies Atlantic, shows air travel has future

ADDITIONAL SUGGESTIONS

1. Give your students many opportunities to practice surveying by itself when they first begin to learn the **survey, read and take notes, review method**. For example, assign a reading, and have your students survey it in class. Then give them a practice quiz about the reading, so they can see how much they have learned from the survey alone! To learn to survey effectively, students need both practice and the opportunity to see the value of this study skill.

2. If the textbook that you use includes "study questions" either in the text itself or at the end of each chapter, engage your students in learning how to use these questions as the focus of their reading and note taking. Help them to see that questions of this sort usually refer to the main ideas and important details in the chapter.

3. Once your students have gained initial mastery of the **survey, read and take notes, review method** for reading textbooks, you may want to begin to teach them flexible reading skills.

    Most students read everything from comic books to the most dense math or science texts at exactly the same speed. This inability to vary reading speed results in highly inefficient and often unsatisfying use of reading time and effort.

    Flexible reading means learning to vary your speed of reading according to (1) the nature of the reading material and how difficult it is for you as a reader, and (2) your purpose for reading it. Reading speeds include skimming and scanning, fast reading, regular reading, and slow reading. People who can read flexibly use their reading time and effort more efficiently and experience greater satisfaction with their reading.

    You will find a more detailed presentation of flexible reading in Unit IX of the **hm Learning and Study Skills Program: Level III**. The materials in this unit can be successfully adapted for students in grades 8-10.

UNIT V SUMMARY: A WAY TO READ TEXTBOOKS

Textbooks are very different from novels, short stories, and plays. Textbooks are written in a special way to help the reader learn the information within them as easily as possible. They are usually organized into chapters and sections, with chapter titles and section headings.

A way of reading textbooks that takes advantage of this organization is the **survey, read and take notes, review method**.

SURVEY	Quickly look over the chapter title, introduction, section headings, and conclusion or summary to get an idea of what the chapter is about. Also, read any questions for study that you find at the end of the chapter.
READ AND TAKE NOTES	Read the chapter carefully. Take notes if you will need to recall the information in the chapter later on.
REVIEW	Go over the main ideas and important details in the chapter. Ask yourself: "What do I need to learn from this reading?" Then answer your question.

UNIT VI
SOLVING PROBLEMS

This unit defines the concept of a problem in a very broad way, which includes situations as seemingly diverse though structurally similar as word problems in mathematics, English papers, and challenging social situations. The key to this concept of a problem is the structural similarity. All of these situations include a starting point, which is a question, conflict, or set of directions, and the need to create an answer or a solution. All of them are problems that can be explored and solved through the use of an organized problem solving method.

This unit presents this broad definition of a problem to your students and then introduces them to a five step method for solving problems.

Of course, problem solving skills are many and varied. This unit is only a first step. We suggest that you involve your students in ongoing instruction in problem solving skills in ways that are relevant to the curriculum of your course.

Please note: In this unit, a strategy is defined as a particular process or method that you employ to find a solution to a problem. It is a way of organizing how you will act. For example, "looking for a pattern" and "making a model" are examples of problem solving strategies. A solution is the answer to the problem. Please be aware of the distinction between these two concepts, and help your students to understand this distinction when it is presented to them in the first activity in this unit.

SUGGESTED DIRECTIONS FOR UNIT VI

1. Introduce this unit by explaining that it will help your students to gain a wider sense of what a problem is as they learn how to solve problems more effectively. Then ask them to read "A 'Party Problem' " (page 40) individually and respond to the question that they are asked. As noted above, you may want to be sure that your students understand the difference between a strategy and a solution.

    Approximate time: 6-9 minutes

2. When they have finished their responses, ask them to share their suggested strategies with the class. List all of the suggestions on the board. When all have been listed, note that you will return to this problem in a few minutes. Have a student read "What Is A Problem?" (page 41) aloud, or read it aloud yourself. Discuss for emphasis.

    6-8 minutes

3. Have your students organize themselves into small groups of three members. If necessary, one or two groups can have two members. Have your students read the directions for Exercise I and work through "Steps One, Two, and Three" (pages 41-42) in their groups. When they have done so, ask each group to share its description of the problem and its selected strategy with the class.

    8-10 minutes

4. Ask your students to read "Step Four" (page 42) and respond to it individually or in their small groups. When they have done so, have several people or groups share their responses. Discuss the nature and variety of the responses.

    8-14 minutes

5. Have your students read "Step Five" (page 43), or have several students read it aloud. Discuss briefly for clarification.

    4-8 minutes

6. Have your students do Exercise II (pages 43-44) in their groups. When they have finished, go over each problem with the class. Focus particularly on the strategies used in solving the problems.

    14-20 minutes

7. Read "Strategies For Problem Solving" (page 45) aloud. Ask your students to do Exercise III (page 46) in their groups. When they have finished, ask them to share their responses. List all of the strategies mentioned on the board. Encourage your students to copy them down. You may want to offer some or all of the following if they are not mentioned:

    look for a pattern   act out the problem
    make a model   construct a table or graph
    work backwards   make a drawing
    restate the problem   solve a simpler problem first
    ask someone else   ignore the problem for a while
    talk it through with someone   free-write about it

    12-18 minutes

8. Have several students read "Some Final Thoughts About Problem Solving" (page 46) aloud. Emphasize the potential value of a feeling or intuition in solving some problems and the need to pay attention to what kind of approach to take with a particular problem. Discuss for clarification.

    6-10 minutes

ANSWERS FOR EXERCISES IN UNIT VI

Pages 41-42, Exercise I

Answers will vary. Engage your students in explaining why they have chosen these particular answers.

Pages 43-44, Exercise II

1. One possible strategy is:

   Number the diagrams #1, #2, and #3 from left to right. Use diagrams #2 and #3 as reference points from which to identify the faces of the block unseen in diagram #1. For example, diagram #1 shows that face b is touched on two sides by faces a and c. Diagram #2 shows that faces e and d touch face b on its other two sides. The face which is opposite face b is none of these, and thus it must be face f.

   Answers: f is opposite b
              c is opposite e
              d is opposite a

2. One possible strategy is:

   Consider why a police officer would signal the driver to stop. The most obvious possibility is speeding. Calculate how fast the truck is going.

   Answer: The truck is speeding.

3. Strategies and answers will vary.

ADDITIONAL ACTIVITIES

1. The most useful follow-up activity to this unit is to engage your students in applying the five step method to the kinds of "problems" that you set for them in your class. The more immediately they use this method in a meaningful context, the more able they will be to use it skillfully and see its values and limitations.

2. You may want to introduce your students to the procedure of brainstorming — listing all of the possible responses to a question, even ones that seem silly or ridiculous, without evaluating any of them until later — as a way of generating a list of possibly useful problem solving strategies in Step Two of the five step problem solving method.

UNIT VI SUMMARY: SOLVING PROBLEMS

A problem is any situation in which you have a starting point, which is a question, conflict, or set of directions, and the need to create a solution or answer. The kinds of problems that you are likely to encounter range from problems in math and science to situations in your life outside school, and everything in between.

One way of solving problems is this five step method:

1. Tell yourself exactly what the problem is. Be clear and specific.

2. Think of at least 2-3 possible strategies that you might use to solve the problem. A strategy is a way or method or process for solving a problem. It's not the answer or solution itself but, rather, how you can find the solution or answer.

3. Examine your list of possible strategies, and choose the one that seems best.

4. Try your best strategy, and see if it works to solve the problem. If it works, you're done!

5. If your best strategy doesn't work, go back to your list of possible strategies in Step Two and choose another. Then try this one.

    Or, stop thinking about the problem for awhile, and come back to it later.

    Or, research the problem, and then start again with Step Two.

Sometimes following an intuition or a feeling can help you solve a problem more effectively than an organized approach like the five step method can.

UNIT VII
HOW DO YOU STUDY?

Unit VII offers the student perhaps the greatest challenge and potential rewards of any unit in the **Program**, as it is designed to engage the student in an exploration of her or his own behavior throughout the studying process. Its goals are:

1) to increase the student's awareness of how she or he learns most effectively,

2) to help the student discover more about what hinders or blocks the effectiveness of her or his learning, and

3) to encourage the student to experiment with creating a learning environment and repertoire of study habits that work well in relation to her or his learning style and family circumstances.

The unit focuses on study environment and study behaviors and strategies. It engages the student in activities that seek to help her or him develop a greater awareness of her or his own study environment and behaviors. Suggested changes that may be of value to the student are offered.

One key to this unit is the concept of learning style. Another is common sense. This unit seeks a creative balance between fostering self-awareness in the student about her or his learning style and suggesting generally useful study behaviors and methods for the student with which the student can experiment.

The underlying theme running throughout this unit is the value of individual experimentation by the student to discover what study methods work best for her or him.

SUGGESTED DIRECTIONS FOR UNIT VII

1. Read the "Introduction" (page 48) and "Study Environment" (page 48) aloud. Ask your students to do Exercise I (page 48). When they are done, have a student read "What Is A Good Study Environment?" (page 49) aloud. Then ask your students to do Exercise II (page 49).

   Approximate time: 8-14 minutes

2. Have your students share their responses to Exercise II with the class. List the suggestions on the board as they are presented. Through a brief discussion and voting process, select the four suggestions that you and the class agree are the most important. Ask your students to note these suggestions in the spaces provided under "Description Of A Good Study Environment" (page 49).

   10-15 minutes

3. Have your students read "Suggestions For Creating A Good Study Environment" (page 50). Discuss these suggestions briefly.

If such a reading would be repetitive of your previous discussion of the aspects of a good study environment, you may want to read aloud only the suggestions that would not be repetitious.

Throughout this discussion, remember that some of your students will not have available to them some or many of the aspects of a "good study environment." You'll want to acknowledge these difficulties and help students consider what they can do, given their family circumstances. For example, sharing a bedroom can make study more difficult. Also, students may not have much control over the noise level in their homes or the kinds of family responsibilities that take up their out-of-school time.

5-10 minutes

4. Have students do Exercise III (page 50). When they have finished, ask them to find a partner and share their responses with each other in pairs. Ask each person to comment on his or her partner's suggested changes.

4-8 minutes

5. Ask your students to do Exercise IV (page 51). When they have completed the exercise, call for a show of hands to see how students rated the method used in the "story." Invite a few students to identify the study method described in the first "story" and explain why they rated the method as they did. Then have a student read aloud the first suggestion in "Suggestions For How To Study" (pages 51-52). Discuss for clarity and emphasis. Repeat this procedure with the other two "stories."

Note that the study method or behavior illustrated in each "story" is discussed in the section in "Suggestions For How To Study" bearing the same number. The same relationship exists between Exercise V and "More Suggestions For How To Study."

12-16 minutes

6. Ask your students to do Exercise V (pages 52-53). When they have finished, have several students share their responses to the question below the first "story." Discuss and evaluate your students' responses. Then have a student read aloud the first suggestion in "More Suggestions For How To Study" (pages 53-54). Discuss for clarity and emphasis. Then repeat this procedure with the other two "stories."

8-14 minutes

ADDITIONAL SUGGESTIONS

1. The activities in this unit are only a beginning towards the achievement of its goals. They offer a step in the right direction but only an initial step. We believe that helping a student discover how he or she can best learn and empowering him or her to act according to such discoveries ought to be a part of any school curriculum. We encourage you to investigate ways through which you can help your students discover more about their own learning styles and to incorporate activities like the ones in this unit into the ongoing curriculum of your classroom.

One way to help your students improve their study behaviors and environment is to ask them questions such as the following ones on a regular basis:

What do you do when you need to understand a difficult homework assignment?

How do you get yourself to do the schoolwork that you need to accomplish?

Do you ever procrastinate with your homework? If so, are you aware of this as you are doing it? How might you be able to stop procrastinating?

Do you turn the tv off when you do your schoolwork? If not, have you tried this out to see what happens when you turn it off? What about your music?

The key to working with these kinds of questions is not to preach to your students but to involve them in reflecting on their own behavior and learning more about what works for them as learners.

UNIT VII SUMMARY: HOW DO YOU STUDY?

Your *study environment* is everything that surrounds you when you study. What's in your *study environment* can have an important effect on your learning.

Be aware of your *study environment:*

1. Choose a place at home to study where you feel comfortable, and study in that place.

2. Try to remove as many distractions as you can from your study environment. A distraction is anything that takes your attention away from your studying.

When you are studying, try to use the following methods:

1. Set goals for how much you want to accomplish during each study session. Try to give yourself an idea of how long each assignment will take.

2. When you start an assignment, quickly tell yourself what you already know about it. Then ask yourself: what am I trying to learn about this? Answer this question.

3. When you finish an assignment, go over what you've just learned. Tell yourself about it as if you were telling another person.

4. Figure out what kinds of studying you do best alone and what you can do well with other people.

5. Find out when you are most awake and alert. Use that time for studying.

6. Try to study for 25-45 minutes at a time. Then take a break for 5-15 minutes before you start again. Reward yourself during the break by doing something that you enjoy.

UNIT VIII
IMPROVING YOUR MEMORY

Throughout their school years, students are required to learn many different kinds of material. Yet they are rarely involved in instruction that can help them understand how learning takes place and how their own memories function.

The purpose of this unit is to help students learn about the workings of human memory and begin to develop several memory skills. Students are introduced to the concepts of short-term and long-term memory and presented with several methods for "moving" information from short-term into long-term memory.

Students are also introduced to several mnemonic methods. Mnemonics is based on scientifically validated principles of how the human memory works. Although mnemonics has been part of our culture for many years, schools have tended to ignore its potential value to students.

If you are not familiar with mnemonics, be sure to examine this unit carefully before you teach it. Try the link method yourself. While this technique is easier for children and adolescents to learn at first, most adults can also learn to use it with practice.

If you would like to learn more about mnemonics in particular and/or memory in general, look at *The Memory Book* by Harry Lorayne and Jerry Lucus (New York: Stein and Day, 1974) or *Your Memory: How It Works* by Kenneth Higbee (Boston: Prentice-Hall/Spectrum, 1977).

Please note: While most of your students in grades 8-10 will be able to visualize or see mental images, a few may not. Don't suggest this possibility at the beginning of the lesson, as the suggestion may negatively influence your students' efforts. Rather, be prepared for the possibility that several students in a class may experience an inability to see mental images. Explain to these students that some part of the population at all ages just doesn't visualize clearly and that recent studies indicate that most people can learn to visualize more clearly through practice.

SUGGESTED DIRECTIONS FOR UNIT VIII

1. Read the directions for "A Memory Game" (page 55) aloud. Ask your students to follow the directions individually. When they have done so, discuss the results of their "playing" the game. Ask questions like the following:

    - For which groups of letters could you remember all of the letters? For which ones couldn't you remember all of the letters?

    - What were the differences between the groups you remembered and the ones you didn't?

    - Can you draw any conclusions based on these differences?

    - Was group #5 different in any way from groups #3 and #6?

Help your students to see that most people can only remember up to nine pieces of information at any moment. If possible, let them discover this conclusion on their own. Also, help them to explore the differences between group #5 and groups #3 and #6.

Approximate time: 6-8 minutes

2. Have your students read "Learning About Memory" (page 56), or have several students read it aloud. Be sure your students understand the nature of short-term and long-term memory.

   6-8 minutes

3. Ask your students to do "Another Memory Game" (page 57) individually. Most students will remember more words from List B than from List A. When they have finished the game, engage them in exploring the differences between the two lists and how this might affect memory.

   6-8 minutes

4. Have your students read "Ways To Remember" (page 58), or read it aloud. Discuss briefly. Then ask your students to read "Ways To Remember: Grouping" (page 58), or read it aloud. Discuss for emphasis. Then ask your students to organize themselves into small groups of 3-4 members. Have them do Exercise I (page 58) in their groups. When the groups have completed the exercise, give each group an opportunity to share one of its "groups of information" with the class. Discuss how grouping can be helpful as a learning skill in your class.

   If your students have difficulty in getting started with this exercise, you may want to give them an example of grouping as it pertains to your curriculum.

   14-20 minutes

5. Have several students read "Ways To Remember: Visualizing" (page 59) aloud. Give your students the opportunity to practice visualizing. Discuss for emphasis. Then have your students read "The Link Method" (pages 59-60) and follow the directions as indicated. Invite them to share their experience in trying the link method with a partner once they have applied the directions to List A. When everyone is ready, discuss the link method for clarification.

   If your students have difficulty with the link method, have them practice with a list of 5-6 words first. Then return to the longer list.

   8-12 minutes

6. Have your students do Exercise II (page 61). When they are finished, discuss their experiences of using the link method a second time.

   6-10 minutes

7. Read "Ways To Remember: Repeating" (page 61) aloud. Invite your students to suggest ways in which they can use this method to help them learn material in your class. Then read "Ways To Remember: Choosing To Remember" (page 61). Ask students to share their reactions to this suggestion.

   6-10 minutes

8. Have your students read "Mnemonics" (page 61) and "Acronyms" (page 62), or have several students read these aloud. Discuss as is useful. Then have your students do Exercise III (page 62) in pairs. When they have finished, go over the exercise. Follow the same procedure for Exercises IV and V (pages 62-63).

12-18 minutes

9. Have your students read "Acrostics" (page 63) and "Other Mnemonic Methods" (page 63). Give your students an opportunity to share any other acrostics that they know with the class.

5 minutes

ANSWERS FOR EXERCISES IN UNIT VIII

Page 62, Exercise III

1. "Homes" is one possible answer.
2. "Roy G. Biv" is one possible answer.

Page 62, Exercise IV

1. absent without leave
2. situation normal, all fouled up

ADDITIONAL SUGGESTIONS

1. A review of the two books cited above as well as other related sources may reveal mnemonic techniques that are particularly relevant to the learning tasks in your subject. An examination of these sources may prove intriguing and useful.

2. One mnemonic method you may find interesting involves the use of peg words. The use of peg words can help you to recall any item on a list without having to run through all of the items on the list prior to the one you are seeking.

   A peg word is a word that stands for a number. Usually it's a word that rhymes with its number. Below you'll find a list of commonly used peg words.

one is a bun	six are sticks
two is a shoe	seven is heaven
three is a tree	eight is a gate
four is a door	nine is a line
five is a hive	ten is a hen

Once you know the peg words, you can use the same mental picturing process that you use in the link method, as follows:

A. Create a mental picture that links the first word in a list with a peg word for one, bun. It helps to use action, proportion, and exaggeration to make the mental picture ridiculous, although you can also use the first image that comes to mind.

B. Next, create a mental image that links the second word in the list to the peg word for two, shoe.

C. Continue this process for all of the words in the list. When you have done so, you'll be able to recall any word in the list according to its number.

3. Creating mapping notes and learning them through visualization is a memory skill that offers much value to students who visualize clearly. You may want to help your students practice this skill in relation to the notes they create for your class.

UNIT VIII SUMMARY: IMPROVING YOUR MEMORY

There are two levels of memory: short-term memory and long-term memory.

— Short-term memory is what you can keep in your attention in the moment. Most people can only remember five to nine different things in their short-term memories.

— Long-term memory is what you know and can bring to mind whenever you choose to do so.

An important part of learning is "moving" information from your short-term memory into your long-term memory. Four ways to accomplish this are:

1. Grouping information

   To group information is to organize it so that details are brought together under the main idea or category that connects them.

2. Visualizing information

   To visualize information is to see an image or picture of it in your mind's eye. For example, you can see a mental picture of an idea or event or an image of your mapping notes.

3. Repeating information

   To repeat information is to put the information in your own words and go over it. Say it aloud to yourself so that you can hear it as well as speak it.

4. Choosing to remember

   The more you choose to remember, the more you will remember. To choose to remember, you need to want to pay attention to and be interested in what you are learning.

Mnemonics is the art of remembering. Mnemonic methods are ways of remembering more efficiently. Three useful mnemonic methods are:

1. The link method

   Link each word in a list with the one following it by creating a picture or image in your mind's eye in which you see objects or events representing both words.

2. Acronym

   An acronym is a word that is made by taking the first letter from each word that you want to remember and making a new word from all of those letters.

3. Acrostic

   An acrostic is a sentence that is made by taking the first letter from each word or symbol that you want to remember and inserting another word beginning with that same letter.

UNIT IX
ORGANIZING THE PARAGRAPH

The complete sentence is the first basic element of good writing. The well-organized paragraph is the second. While students in these grades have had much instruction in writing sentences, often their experience with organizing paragraphs is limited.

The activities in this unit present students with four essential criteria they can use to organize paragraphs that they write and to evaluate the structural effectiveness of those paragraphs. These criteria are the topic sentence, support, unity, and coherence. When students learn to use these criteria as they write, they develop not only composition skills but also a number of essential thinking skills related to the organization and clear presentation of a position or argument.

The last activity in the unit presents students with a specific process that they can use for organizing and writing paragraphs.

This unit is designed to engage your students in a discovery process concerning the criteria for elements of a good paragraph. Its activities relate to each other as follows:

> Paragraph A in "The Paragraph Detective" (page 65) lacks a topic sentence. The first section in "What Are The Elements Of A Good Paragraph?" (page 66) deals with the topic sentence, as does Exercise I (page 66) which follows it. The three other criteria/elements are presented in the same way.

SUGGESTED DIRECTIONS FOR UNIT IX

1. Have your students do Part I of "The Paragraph Detective" (page 65). Go over their responses orally, writing the "correct" answers on the board in the language used by the students.

    Approximate time: 8-10 minutes

2. Have a student read "What Is A Paragraph?" (page 66) aloud, or read it aloud yourself. Then read aloud "Topic Sentence" from "What Are The Elements Of A Good Paragraph?" (page 66). Discuss briefly, relating this element to Paragraph A of "The Paragraph Detective." Ask your students to do Exercise I (page 66). Go over the exercise orally. Have several students read "correct" answers to show the potential for a variety of good topic sentences for the same paragraph.

    8-12 minutes

3. Follow the same procedure for "Support" (page 66) as you did for "Topic Sentence." After you have read "Support," have your students read the "Example Paragraph" (page 67). Have them pick out the details and examples that support the topic sentence. Then follow the same procedure for Exercise II (page 67) as you did for Exercise I.

    6-10 minutes

4. Follow the same procedure for Part II of "The Paragraph Detective" (page 68) as you did for Part I.

8 -12 minutes

5   Follow the same procedure for "Unity" and Exercise III (page 69) and "Coherence" (page 69) and Exercise IV (page 69) as you did for "Topic Sentence" and Exercise I.

12-18 minutes

6. Ask your students to read "A Way To Organize Paragraphs" (page 70). Discuss each step for emphasis and clarity. Then ask your students to do Exercise V (page 71). When they have finished, ask several volunteers to write their outlines on the board. Discuss and evaluate.

The topic listed in Exercise V is a suggested topic. You may find that your students are more responsive to an alternative topic. Or, you may choose to use a topic that relates directly to the ongoing curriculum of your class.

15-25 minutes

ANSWERS FOR EXERCISES IN UNIT IX

Pages 65, 68

The Paragraph Detective

A. No topic sentence
B. Lacks support for topic sentence
C. Lacks unity
D. Lacks coherence

Page 66

Exercise I

Accept any appropriate answers. One example is:
>   In the nineteen fifties, rock and roll was a new kind of popular music.

Page 67

Exercise II

Accept any appropriate answer. Two examples are:

>   Figure skating is probably my favorite sport. I started cross-country skiing
>   two years ago and enjoy it almost as much as skating.

Page 69

Exercise III

Sentences 3, 6, 11

Exercise IV

Sentences 8, 9, 10

ADDITIONAL SUGGESTIONS

1. Once your students have become adept at recognizing and writing topic sentences that appear at the beginning of the paragraph, give them practice in recognizing and writing topic sentences that have other positions within a paragraph.

2. Give your students the opportunity to use the criteria of support, unity, and coherence to evaluate other paragraphs: their own, each others, or examples you provide for them.

UNIT IX SUMMARY: ORGANIZING THE PARAGRAPH

The two basic building blocks of good writing are the complete sentence and the paragraph.

A paragraph is a group of sentences that are organized around one main idea.

The elements of a good paragraph are:

1.	Topic sentence	A sentence that clearly states what the paragraph is about, usually placed at the beginning of the paragraph.
2.	Support	Details and examples that describe, back up, or explain the topic sentence.
3.	Unity	All of the sentences are directly related to the main idea expressed in the topic sentence.
4.	Coherence	Each sentence follows the one before it in a way that makes sense.

Writing good paragraphs begins with organizing your ideas. You can use the method described below to organize your ideas before you write, and then write a paragraph.

1. First, think about what you want to say.

2. Write down the main idea of the paragraph. Then jot down the details and examples that you want to include under it. This will give you a working outline.

3. Take your main idea and write it as a topic sentence. Then, using your outline as a guide, write the rest of the paragraph.

4. Read over what you've written and check for support, unity, and coherence.

UNIT X
PREPARING FOR AND TAKING TESTS:
OBJECTIVE QUESTIONS

The purpose of testing is to determine what students have learned. Too often students' ability to communicate their learning is hampered by their lack of skills for preparing for and taking tests.

Most teacher-made tests allow for the student to gain a great deal by effective preparation. A part of this unit introduces your students to several methods by which they can make more effective use of the time and energy they devote to preparing for a test.

Test questions of all kinds ask students to organize and communicate their knowledge and understanding in particular ways. Each kind of question requires its own skills for students to convey what they know about the question through the format of that question. The skills involved in understanding the various test questions and the kinds of answers they require are called "testwiseness." The more "testwise" students are, the more able they will be to demonstrate what they know through the format of a test. Much of this unit is designed to help students begin to develop "testwiseness" for objective questions. In Unit XI, students will work with related skills for essay questions.

While growing numbers of teachers are using performance-based assessments in secondary school classrooms, students are still likely to experience many tests that include objective questions.

SUGGESTED DIRECTIONS FOR UNIT X

1. Have your students read "How Do You Prepare For A Test?" (page 73) and describe how they would prepare for a test. Then have them read "Preparing For A Test" (page 73). Be sure they know that they will refer to what they have written here later in the unit.

    Approximate time: 6-8 minutes

2. Have students read aloud "Test Questions" (page 73), "What Are Objective Questions?" (page 74), and "What Can You Learn About Objective Questions That Will Be Helpful?" (page 74). Or, have students read these sections by themselves. Discuss briefly for clarification and emphasis.

    6-8 minutes

3. Read "Multiple Choice," including "How To Answer Multiple Choice Questions" (page 75) aloud, or have students read it aloud. Complete the example orally, modeling the process described in the section above it. Discuss briefly. Then ask your students to do Exercise I (page 76) within a given time limit (2-3 minutes). When they have finished, go over the exercise orally, and ask students to describe the processes they used to determine their answers.

    You may want to have students work in pairs as they do this exercise and several or all of the similar ones in this unit. If so, be sure to give students a little more time in which they can discuss their responses and reach agreement.

    8-12 minutes

4. Ask your students to read "Narrowing Down The Choices" (page 77). When they have done so, discuss the process suggested and the criteria that are appropriate for your tests. Then have your students do Exercise II (page 78). When they are finished, go over the exercise orally, asking students to share the process they used to "narrow down." You may want to have students develop some of their own multiple choice questions in small groups and apply the "narrowing down" skills to these questions, for example, with groups exchanging questions.

8-12 minutes

5. Use a similar procedure with "Matching" (page 79), the Example (page 79), and Exercise III (page 79).

You may want to offer the following additional suggestions for matching questions:

a. Look over all of the choices, because sometimes there's a better match than the first possible match that you find.

b. If you're having trouble working from the left column to the right, try reversing it and working from the right column to the left.

c. Make sure that you use each letter only once, unless otherwise directed.

d. Read the directions carefully. Sometimes you may be asked to match opposites. Other times you may be allowed to use a letter more than once.

8-16 minutes

6. Have a student read "Short Answers" (page 80) aloud. Have your students do Exercise IV (page 80), or replace Exercise IV with several short answer questions that relate directly to the curriculum of your class. When students have finished, go over the exercise orally.

4-6 minutes

7. Read "True/False Questions" (page 80) aloud. Go over the Example (page 80) orally. You may want to discuss in particular questions that include the words *all*, *always*, *only*, and *never*. Then ask your students to do Exercise V (page 81). Tell them that they may check their own answers when they have finished by turning to pages 82-83. When your students have completed answering the questions and checking their answers, go over each suggestion in the "Answers" (pages 82-83) orally. Discuss each suggestion for clarification and emphasis. Involve students in applying these suggestions to their own studying experience.

10-20 minutes

8. Ask your students to do Exercise VI (page 83). When they have finished, have them form small groups of three members and share their responses with each other in their groups. You may also want to follow the small group sharing with a short class discussion focusing on ways to prepare for a test.

8-14 minutes

ANSWERS FOR EXERCISES IN UNIT X

Page 75
Example: E

Page 76
Exercise I
1. A
2. E
3. C
4. B
5. C

Page 78
Example: B, C
Exercise II
1. A, B, C, E
2. B, C, D, E (Some students may not be able to eliminate B.)
3. A, C, E
4. Students may not be able to eliminate any choices, as both B and C may seem plausible.

Page 79
Example: 6   hands
                    4   spinnerets
                    5   wings
                    1   paws
                    3   mane
                    2   pouch
Exercise III
                    6   Maine
                    7   Texas
                    5   Louisiana
                    1   Illinois
                    8   California
                    3   Idaho
                    2   New York
                    4   Oklahoma

Page 80
Exercise IV
                    1. eight
                    2. They sailed across the Atlantic Ocean in ships.
                    3. left
Example: 1. false
                    2. false

Page 81
Exercise V
Answers on pages 82-83

ADDITIONAL SUGGESTIONS

1. If you use other kinds of objective questions on the tests you give (for example, word problems; you can find suggestions for teaching "testwiseness" skills related to word problems in the **hm Math Study Skills Program**), engage your students in exercises like the ones in this unit in relation to those kinds of questions. This will help your students to familiarize themselves with the workings of these kinds of questions.

2. Inform your students of your policy about guessing on tests in your classroom. Help them to understand when it is helpful to guess and when it is not.

3. You may use test items for which students must discriminate between two or more correct choices and select a best choice if they are to gain credit. If you do, you will probably want to model this process for your students and help them learn not just to pick the first correct answer but to search through all of the choices for the best answer.

4. You may wish to familiarize your students with the kinds of test questions used on standardized tests. Being "testwise" can make a considerable difference for students on tests of this sort. For example, with practice, students can become more skillful at correctly completing the kinds of word analogies that appear on the SAT.

UNIT X SUMMARY: PREPARING FOR AND TAKING TESTS: OBJECTIVE QUESTIONS

Objective questions usually have one correct answer for which you will receive credit.

There are four main kinds of objective questions. You can learn methods for answering them that will help you on a test.

The four main kinds of objective questions are:

1. Multiple Choice — Read the question carefully. Try to think of the answer before you look at the choices. Read all of the choices given. If you don't know the answer after you've read the choices, use a process of elimination. Cross off the choices you know to be wrong. Pick the most sensible one that remains. When you can, use information in the question itself to help you narrow down the choices.

2. Matching — Do the ones you know first, and cross them off. Then do the best you can with whatever ones are left.

3. Short Answer — If you don't know the exact answer, write down anything you do know that's related. You may get partial credit.

4. True/False — Read the statements very carefully. Remember that all parts of a statement must be true for the statement to be true.

How you prepare for a test has a lot to do with how well you'll do on it. The more skillfully you prepare, the better you'll do.

UNIT XI
PREPARING FOR AND TAKING TESTS:
ESSAY QUESTIONS

This unit familiarizes students with the nature of essay questions and introduces them to a method for answering these questions. Its activities are designed to help students gain a better understanding of how essay questions work and a greater sense of control over the way that they prepare for and respond to essay questions.

The best follow-up to this unit is to give students an opportunity to apply what they have learned to answering essay questions on a test in your classroom. You may want to schedule this unit so that it shortly precedes a test that includes essay questions. If you do, be sure to give your students feedback not only on what they have written in their essays but also on how they have used the skills presented in this unit.

SUGGESTED DIRECTIONS FOR UNIT XI

1. Read aloud "Answering Essay Questions" (page 85) and "What Is An Essay Question?" (page 85), or have students read it aloud. Discuss briefly for emphasis. You may want to review the steps for organizing a paragraph with the class.

    Approximate time: 5-8 minutes

2. Have students read "A Method For Writing Answers To Essay Questions: Before The Test and When You First Get The Test" (page 86). Discuss for emphasis. Invite students to add any related suggestions. Then ask them to read "How To Organize Your Essay" (page 87). Discuss the purpose of each of the steps suggested.

    8-14 minutes

3. Ask students to do Exercise I (page 88). When they have finished their outlines, have them form small groups of 3-4 members and share their outlines with each other. Ask them to give each other feedback as to how clear their outlines are and whether they include main ideas and supporting details.

    Please note: You may want to replace the "essay question" included in Exercise I with a question that is more relevant to your class or course.

    10-12 minutes

4. Read aloud "How To Begin Your Essay" (page 89), or have a student read it aloud. Discuss for emphasis. Then read aloud "How To Use Your Time" (page 89). Discuss briefly.

    6-10 minutes

5. Have a student read aloud the first two paragraphs in "What Words Are Used To Ask Essay Questions?" (page 90). Then engage your students in articulating a clear definition for each word listed. Let them get as close as they can to the correct definition, and then give them assistance as needed. The more the definitions can be in your students' own words, the more helpful they will be to your students. Write the correct definitions on the board, and ask your students to copy them in their student texts on page 90.

An alternative would be to organize your students into groups and to ask each group to create the best definitions it can for each word. Then have the groups share their definitions, and help students to develop one accurate definition for each word, as much as possible in their own words.

If you use other words to ask essay questions, add them to the list and help your students define them in the same way.

8-12 minutes

6. Have your students read "More Suggestions For Writing Essay Answers" (page 91). Discuss briefly. Then ask your students to read "What Can You Do When A Test Is Returned To You?" (page 91) and answer the question. Invite students to share their answers with the class. Stress the idea that you can learn a good deal both about the content of a test and about how to take a test when you look over your corrected test paper.

6-10 minutes

SUGGESTED DEFINITIONS FOR WORDS USED
TO ASK ESSAY QUESTIONS

1. describe   - to convey an impression or account of something, usually without judging it; or, to tell about what something is, for example, describing a person or a place.

2. summarize - to give a brief statement of the main points, usually without judging those points.

3. compare   - to show the similarities and differences between two or more things.

4. contrast   - to show the differences between two or more things.

5. explain   - to make clear the cause or reason for something.

6. evaluate   - to weigh positive and negative evidence about something and give your opinion based on the evidence.

7. criticize   - to make judgments as to the correctness or value of something.

8. discuss   - to explore the arguments for and against something.

ADDITIONAL SUGGESTIONS

1. You may wish to require your students to include a brief outline as well as completed essays in response to essay questions on tests. When you do this, be sure to give credit for the outline.

    This practice can be seen as analogous to "showing your work" on a math problem and will encourage students to think through their essay answers before they write them.

2. Have students predict essay questions that will be included on tests. Give bonus points if student predictions are accurate.

3. You may wish to provide your students with "suggested times" for each essay question given. Gradually, as students become more adept at pacing themselves, you can wean them away from this support.

4. You may wish to engage your students in instruction and practice that helps them learn how to include enough details to support the main points that they make in their essay answers.

PLEASE NOTE: Unit XII, "Using Your Time," begins with a homework assignment that students must complete prior to the class period during which the unit is taught.

UNIT XI SUMMARY: PREPARING FOR AND TAKING TESTS: ESSAY QUESTIONS

An essay question asks you to organize what you know and understand about a topic and to express it in a way that responds to that particular question. You need to organize your essay answer around main ideas and include important details that support these main ideas.

You can use the same method for organizing and writing your answer to an essay question that you used for writing paragraphs. You'll need to work more quickly when you're taking a test, but the method is well worth using.

Below are the steps in the method:

1. Read the essay question carefully. Then think about what you want to say in response to the question.

2. Jot down a brief outline of your answer.

3. Begin your essay answer with a thesis statement that states the main ideas of your answer. A thesis statement is like a topic sentence for your answer.

4. Then write your answer.

5. If you have time, read over your essay and make any necessary changes or corrections.

To answer essay questions well, you need to understand the special words that teachers use t o ask these questions. Some of these words are: describe, summarize, compare, contrast, explain, evaluate, criticize, and discuss.

UNIT XII
USING YOUR TIME

As does Unit VII, this unit engages your students in an exploration of an aspect of their own behavior. In this case, it is the students' use of time. The activities in this unit help students to look carefully at how they have used the time available on a given school day. Then the concept and procedure of scheduling is introduced to them, and students are given the opportunity to create, use, and evaluate a daily schedule and/or a weekly schedule.

Some of your students may be resistant to the concept of scheduling, as they may perceive it as an infringement of their freedom. It is important that you be sensitive to this possibility. The purpose of this unit is *not* to train all students to use a schedule. Rather, it is intended to offer the tool of a schedule to those young people who are interested in learning how to use it. For those of your students who find scheduling helpful, you may want to offer follow-up instruction beyond this unit.

Note that two kinds of schedules are introduced in this unit. It is helpful to stress to your students that one kind of schedule may be more useful to an individual than the other kind.

Your students will probably vary widely in terms of the amount of choice they have over their use of time. Family situations and responsibilities can promote or limit the degree of control that young people have over their own time. In the course of this unit, you may want to acknowledge this factor and discuss it as is appropriate for your class. Students may want to discuss with you or among themselves their desires for rearranging some aspects of their schedules in their families. Your input can be of value in this kind of discussion, given your recognition of your dual responsibility to your students and to their parents.

SUGGESTED DIRECTIONS FOR UNIT XII

1. Have your students complete the "Assignment Before Class" (pages 93-96) and "Learning From Your Record Of A School Day" (page 97) and bring their records and answers to class on the appropriate day.

   If your students are interested, have them track three days rather one, as three days will give them a more complete picture of their time use. If students track their activities for three days, have them calculate an average for each relevant category in "Learning From Your Record Of A School Day" (page 97).

2. Ask two or three students to volunteer to copy their "Record Of A School Day" (page 94) on the board. While they are doing this, have the rest of the class read the "Introduction" (page 98) and "What Should You Keep In Mind When You Are Creating A Schedule?" (page 98). Or, have students read these sections aloud.

   Approximate time: 5-7 minutes

3.   Discuss the "Records" on the board. Consider them in terms of the following:

A.   How did this day feel to the person? For example: Good? Rushed? Frustrating?

B.   How much time was given to each activity? Too much or too little? Enough?

C.   What time of day was chosen for each activity? Why?

D.   Was the allocation of time a good one both in terms of how much and which part of the day?

When you have explored each "Record," discuss the following questions:

A.   How do you decide how much time to give to an activity?

B.   How do you decide when to do something?

15-20 minutes

4.   Have your students read "Creating A Schedule" (page 99), or read it aloud. Discuss for clarification. Then have your students follow the directions and create a "daily schedule." Tell them to go ahead and read "Using Your Schedule: What Happened?" (page 102) when they have finished drawing up their own schedules.

Remind your students to use pencil for this exercise so they can make changes easily.

Some of your students may find it difficult to create a daily schedule because some of the regular events in their lives, such as meals, take place at different times on different days. You may need to acknowledge and discuss this possibility.

Time needed will vary, depending on students' prior experience.

5.   There are two options as to how to proceed from here:

A.   Ask your students to follow the "Daily Schedule" they have created for the next school day and to respond to the questions in "Using Your Schedule" in writing. Ask your students to bring their responses to class on the day after the one that they schedule. In class, have your students form small groups of 3-4 members and share their experiences of using a schedule. Then gather the whole class and continue this discussion. You may want to collect the **Programs**, go over the students' responses on page 102, and report to the class the next day about the nature of their experience as a whole.

Have your students read "Creating A Weekly Schedule" (page 103), or read it aloud. Discuss the differences between a daily and a weekly schedule. Invite your students to try using a weekly schedule like the example on page 104.

End the class by having a student read "Using A Schedule: A Few Last Words" (page 103) aloud. Discuss for emphasis.

B. Have your students read "Creating A Weekly Schedule" (page 103), or have a student read it aloud. Discuss for clarification. Then give your students the choice of (1) following the daily schedule they have already drawn up, or (2) creating a weekly schedule like the one on page 104 and using it for a week. Ask both groups to respond to the questions in "Using Your Schedule" in writing. Have each student let you know which option she or he has chosen. End the class by having a student read "Using A Schedule: A Few Last Words" (page 103) aloud. Discuss for emphasis.

On the appropriate day a week later, ask your students to bring their daily or weekly schedules to class along with their responses to "Using Your Schedule." Involve them in considering their experiences with a schedule in the ways described in option A.

6. A second weekly schedule form is included for additional practice.

ADDITIONAL SUGGESTIONS

1. If your students express resistance to the concept of scheduling, you may be able to lower their resistance by stressing the idea that their schedule belongs to them and they have the power to make it and change it.

2. One way to illustrate the value of schedules is to ask parents to share their own time management systems with their children, either individually at home or through a few parent presentations in class. One tool that has increasing use is an electronic planner. You may have one of your own that you can demonstrate, or find a parent who can offer this presentation. Another common planning tool is a weekly calendar; you may wish to demonstrate how these work.

3. Students may benefit from copying their weekly schedule and keeping it in their notebooks and/ or lockers.

4. If many or most of your students begin to use schedules, you'll want to help them evaluate their use of these tools on a regular basis, at least in the first weeks and months of use.

UNIT XII SUMMARY: USING YOUR TIME

A *schedule* is a plan that you create for how you want to spend your time. A good schedule can help you do both what you must do and what you want to do.

When you make a schedule for yourself, keep the following ideas in mind:

1. Try to make each day a "balanced" one, giving yourself time for both work and play.

2. Figure out when you are most awake and alert, and try to do your studying then.

3. Try to spend at least some time during each school day studying. If you have no homework due the next day, work on long-term projects.

One kind of schedule is a daily schedule. Another kind is a weekly schedule.

The purpose of any schedule that you make for yourself is to help you organize your time better, so you can do what you want and need to do.